The Fire's Edge

poems by

Nancy Richardson

Finishing Line Press
Georgetown, Kentucky

The Fire's Edge

Copyright © 2017 by Nancy Richardson
ISBN 978-1-63534-129-4 First Edition
All rights reserved under International and Pan-American Copyright Conventions.
No part of this book may be reproduced in any manner whatsoever without written permission from the publisher, except in the case of brief quotations embodied in critical articles and reviews.

ACKNOWLEDGMENTS

Thank you to the editors of the following books and journals where several of these poems have appeared.

Dogwood: "In the Cardiologist's Office"
Mobius: "Kent State Trial, 1975"

The following poems have appeared in the chapbook, *Unwelcomed Guest*, published by the Main Street Rag Publishing Company, 2013: "In the Cardiologist's Office, "On the Street Where You Live," "Kent State Trial," "Fathers," "Undercover Letter Dates," and "Mayflies."

Publisher: Leah Maines

Editor: Christen Kincaid

Cover Art: John Anderson

Author Photo: Judy Brook

Cover Design: John Anderson

Printed in the USA on acid-free paper.
Order online: www.finishinglinepress.com
also available on amazon.com

Author inquiries and mail orders:
Finishing Line Press
P. O. Box 1626
Georgetown, Kentucky 40324
U. S. A.

Table of Contents

Randomness 1
Fainting 2
Shale Play 3
Patience 4
Returning to Kent State 5
High School Reunion 6
Fear 7
Clarence and Anita 8
Undercover Dates 9
Spinning 10
Volunteers 11
On the Street 12
Kent State Trial 13
Door to Door 14
The Fire's Edge 15
The Paralegal 16
Cake in His Head 17
Lines 18
The Blue Trail 19
Fathers 20
The Accident 21
Listening 22
Untying 23
Lost 24
Say 25
Later 26
Pay Dirt 27
In the Cardiologist's Office 28
Mayflies 29

*For my sister, Galen Keller Lewis,
researcher for the Kent State Trial
and advocate for the thirteen students
shot or killed at Kent State.*

Randomness
Kent State, 1970

She slid from her bed on the morning of May 4,
chose the bright red blouse for the occasion
of the day of her death. Sometimes I wonder
how my death will come specifically the *like*,
the *what*, the *how*. Will it be after dinner I rise
from the table, grab the hot wire of an infarct
across my chest, or after the tenth visit to
the cancer clinic where the vile brew delivered
through the pic-line turns my skin yellow, then blue,
then white. But getting back to her as she slammed
the screen door, smelled the newly cut grass, walked
looking up at the pillowed clouds and the man pointing
the gun four hundred feet away saw something
extraordinary through his sight. A dazzling red and gold
flash moving in the parking lot. A small sun come
to the tarred surface. I rise from my bed and offer to the gods
of randomness *maybe, perhaps, if*: life as hypothetical.

Fainting

I fainted idiopathically, which means the cause was not apparent. Heart accelerated, free agent of pace and rhythm beating against my chest wall, room tilting, legs soft, noodling. Then adult faces hovering, small helicopters of concern. I remembered only the sound of falling cutlery, a band playing, voices calling from far, far away. But those lost unconscious moments exist somewhere in the cosmos, owed to me by the fact I have not lived them. *This is the time for sleep says the insomnia tape, the time to release your thoughts. You can find them again but for now let them just slide over the horizon.* You will find them again, those unthought thoughts, those unlived moments. Out there waiting just over the horizon where the insomniacs, the lost, the unconscious have left them. Before their bodies gave up their minds. Before they entered the deep dark and peaceful place and let them go.

Shale Play

In the Hampton Inn beside the skeleton of the steel mills,
men in T-shirts drink their coffee before injecting chemicals
ten thousand feet below the ground, fracturing the gray shale.
In the lobby dining space yogurt cups sweat in ice
and scrambled eggs quiver in the metal pan. The parking lot is full.
A billionaire is planning to develop Mars-terrafirm lanscapes,
pink hotels, associated industries and iron-oxide sunsets.
Red planet evacuation site. Here in the Ohio motel
where the breakfast mess is being cleaned up, the men have left
to pump black ooze. Trickling in after five they'll wash
the guar, benzene, dioxane from their boots—amble to the bar.

Patience
The voting machines of Ohio.

The poor breathe the quiet air of corruption
in the gymnasium where the voting machines sit,
stout, winking hulks. The screens dissolve in a storm
of snow. Votes float into errant flying digits.
Patience festers at the edge of the freeway.
Resignation waits in long lines.
The power brokers, riding cheap tricks
say cheating in the service of liberty is no vice.

Returning to Kent State
> *In its countless alveoli space contains compressed time.*
> *That is what space is for.* —Gaston Bachelard

In the grassy courtyard of the married student housing,
Derek and the Dominoes blasts in blue moonlight,
Layla you've got me on my knees. Just up the hill
voices from the Tri-Towers dorm float downwind,
can't stand it anymore. We feel the bullet holes
in the brick walls as we pass by. On the hill
the metal sculpture, another bullet hole, small tunnel
on the way to flesh. Pause and turn to see
the scattered bodies in still poses, in memory
lying in the grassy meadow. Daniel Berrigan
marching, just out of jail his hair flecked gray.
The scent of candle wax, low voices murmuring.
Bill Schroeder's parents standing in his spot
in the shadow of a tree, candlelight casting
shadows on their strained pale faces.

High School Reunion

I open the Holiday Inn event room door to bodies
in advanced stages of jowls, paunches clutching
one another grateful to have escaped the departed
on page one of the program. The preacher
in the purple silk suit and top hat thanks God
for the entire history between then and now.
Elvis's bodyguard's ex-wife flashes
her 21 carat diamond ring at the gifted,
who are talking achievement and other theories
of success, while the abused classmate's husband
stares fists at me. The palm reader with the long brown hair
and lipsticked smile says, " I have had a fascinating life."

Fear
> *Kent State gymnasium, 1970*

The air is thick with strobe lights and sweat.
On stage Jefferson Airplane sings for the four dead

and the nine wounded. Gracie Slick in a voice
like a dirt road, *we are outlaws in the eyes*

of America, tear down the walls. Behind her on the screen
Jeffrey Miller's body leaking down the concrete in blue

staccato lights. Somewhere a door lets in a gust of fear.
Tear down the walls won't you try?

But trying's getting ready to run in fear's leather boots.
I scream, punching the blue mist.

Clarence and Anita on the Way to the Seminar

When Clarence got into my car he slid
into the back seat waiting for Anita
to hurry it up. Anita chose the front.
On her face an expression
that every woman knows-
a little fear, a little anger, halfway
wanting to please. Being desired
and disrespected at the same time.
A king in his carriage
in the car on the way to the seminar.
I drove and Anita sighed, the two of us
in service to his ambition
weaved through D.C. traffic as he grunted
and rustled the New York Times.

Undercover Letter Dates
At Kent State 1972

The writer had long talks with Jann Wenner on the phone.
Wrote a profile of Nelson Algren for Rolling Stone.
Said his father was a magician who locked the pigeons
and rabbits in a room and went away. Strange noises
and feathers followed. One day I passed a desk in
Taylor Hall, his name carved in the wood: N. A. R. C.

Another said he was an education student.
Wanted to do a project with me. Take me to a meeting
in D.C. His tailpipe fell off as we drove
down the avenue, loud noises and sparks flying.
In the index of Michener's book his name,
next to it: N. S. A.

Spinning

He skidded off a black silk rope of road
into a gulley, perhaps braking
for some small animal in his headlights,
slamming metal, velocity downward.
Someone said there are endless possibilities
in life, spin and choose. I don't believe it.
Each moment's intentions are held
in weak arms. Just before he slid,
the air was white and there were two roads out.
Hesitate, or ride over the soft edge,
brake, or run the damn thing over.

Volunteers of America

We are here to save democracy
where the clouds are soot
where street money flows
and the ceiling leaks toilet water.
Workers are gathered
with their earnest faces.
We say some doors
are too dangerous to knock on
even in daylight.
Take off your jewelry.

On the Street Where You Live

The squat and menacing man behind the chain
link fence with the slicked hair and a ten dollar bill
says, "here kids, go and get some ice cream," in a tone
that means *ya gotta go and now*. In the background
Vic Damone croons, *I don't care if I can be here
on the street where you live* to the Mafia Don's
daughter, with whom his engagement lasts two months.
Does enchantment pour out of every door?
Guests mingle. This is 1948, twelve years before
the bombings and before Bobby Kennedy calls it
Murder Town. Before the poor man's urban renewal
known as arson. Before the demolition.

Kent State Trial, 1975

"The photos speak for themselves," says the Judge
to the students' lawyers. The jury puzzles over them,
but the photos lose their nerve. In one
the Governor shouts, "worse than the brown-shirts
and the communists, night riders and the vigilantes."
Or another, blue sky, clouds, a clot of guardsmen
huddles in the field, as though for a picnic on a day
in May. If this photo could listen it might overhear
their plans to turn in unison and fire. But it is busy
and the guardsmen are whispering. Here now tongues
should be wagging, "the guardsmen turn
and level their weapons," and "the guardsmen shoot.
All together now. Fire!" But the words are prisoners
in their cells, banging their tin cups against the metal bars.
The photos go on in silence, in cardboard boxes
in wet basements. The photos hold their tongues.

Door to Door

Let these people
not be home

let the flyers
blow away quietly

stick to the
chain link fences

let me not walk up
these concrete steps,
one more time

stand on this torn
green outdoor rug

read the Persuasion Script
promise life

will get better
perhaps not now

perhaps in some
other person's lifetime

The Fire's Edge

The Portland taxi wheels crunch on gravel
and I touch her as our reflections bleed down
the wet window glass. I will not see her again.
Sisters, we were born on the fire's edge
in a town of sulfur dust, metal water. At night
we sweated the uphill climb to see
the open hearth's unholy glow on the horizon.
In the old mattress with the sinking center
we talked of our futures and who would love us.
The screen door slaps. I turn, see the window,
her face melting in watercolor light.

The Paralegal

> *I was to keep her sitting next to me*
> *at the counsel table depending on her infallibility*
> *in retrieving facts.*   —Joseph Kelner

She sits on the floor,
rifles through the box
of evidence, manila folders,
fading photographs,
looking for something
about a conspiracy,
something about
who set the fire.
The one thing
that might have made
the difference.
And she gazes out
at the fogbound trees,
the endless rain.

Cake in His Head

Sitting in the stage light,
the strings of the guitar
moving with his fingers,
brown hair falling
over his handsome left eye,
he seemed the perfect cake.
But inside an ingredient
was missing and the batter
had collapsed. He couldn't
be extracted from the pan
except in pieces. Each misshapen
piece a puzzle on the plate.

Lines

I'll always love you.
I told her to stay away.
I just have to check with some people.
I have to go back into the office to sort through some things.
That's just powdered sugar.
What do you mean, I spend a lot of time in the bathroom.
We just had a drink.
I want to go over your thesis with you.
The trouble is I don't know how much.
I never sleep with my patients.

The Blue Trail

cold air hits my face
my feet stumble on tree roots
the sun is strained through trees
my chest hurts from cold
look the jewel weed flower
freezes on the stem
the pond is coming up
how still the lily pads
are turning brown
I try not to think of you
I meet a group of women
with their dogs
on the blue trail
we toss sticks into the pond
I worry that the water is too cold
you must have reminded me
of someone

Fathers

Once when we were twelve, playing
cards in my living room, she whispered,
my father comes to me in the night.
She said, *first the footsteps, then
his hands.* She learned to float
above herself, look down on the bed.
And I, my father having left us,
thought this must be what fathers do.
Make you leave your life or push you
from your body. Daughters hovering
waiting for the sheets to be quiet,
or at the window looking
down the street for his walk,
his pale hands reaching out for you.

The Accident
> *The secret of this journey is to let the wind*
> *blow its dust all over your body*   —James Wright

He said hold on but he slipped,
fell from my hands.
I find him again and again
in the dream, standing
in the back of the room,
leaning against the wall.
I make my way to him
through rows of folding chairs,
each one a small metallic barrier.
I reach him and he will say:
This journey is full of dust.
We fall through our own lives.

Listening

To those reel-to-reel tapes,
Lou Reed, Jimi Hendrix
and the Messiah, outlier
winding its way toward
*Worthy is the Lamb
who was slain.* I would find
you again then, body
re-gathering its cells,
standing in the dark, soft eyes,
long brown hair.
This winter in a church
filled with light,
the words returned in a chorus,
glistening violins and voices.
Long years ago I listened
for one last configuration
in the plastic spinning tapes.
*He shall stand at the latter day
upon the earth.* Night after night
the curtains lifting in a slight breeze,
the moon and *forever and ever. Amen.*

Untying

The motorcyclist, wooly blond
soft skin, left me
with a midnight phone call
breathing silence.
The painter of orange abstracts
pausing in mid-sentence,
moved to the coast of Nova Scotia
where he sent for me in letters.
There were others. Some right
at the wrong time. Some wrong
for all time. I carry their voices
in my ear, their whispers
borne like the dead.
Small knots in the brain.
I untie them.

Lost

I am lost in the woods following a dead end trail,
my ability to bushwhack up the steep hill in front of me
in doubt. Sit down, ponder the lost path. I sit in a patch of moss
and think. This wandering. Getting old. Mr. Kinney lived to be 90.
Did his work. Then said, "I'm all used up," and died.
And what about the sky? Look up. Voyager, star ship wandering
in space for 35 years doing its own work. Photographing
the rings of Saturn, the volcanoes of Venus, the moons, Io, Delphi.
Voyager has just entered the heliosphere, a space
where there is no reach of sun, no solar wind, only remnants of stars
millions of year old. Into the quiet zone of no wind. Work done,
battery depleted, no return. This is where all journeys will end,
in a place of windless spirit particles. The sun hits the spruces,
red pines. Breath coming back, body heat down from cool moss.
I get up. Retrace the steps on the trails marked Slough,
Circumferential Dell. Find the intersection where I went wrong.
Where I chose the dead end path. There it is. Hidden in green.
Fern Walk, the path I came in on.

Say

The slant light of winter
through tall windows
where music plays.
We make bird-houses,
read stories, eat fruit.
Their small eyes stare up
into my safe face, not a face
attached to smacking hands.
Hands that would make you want
to take your clothes off,
rub grease in your hair,
jump out the window.
I sit across from each child,
say, *look at me—this is a red apple,*
say *apple,* say *water,*
this is water. Say,
I will remember you.

Later

In the vineyard garden
of green moss, slender trees
and the bamboo fountain's shush,
the six of us talk of you
as you would have been
in this moment. But the wine
glasses clink and voices sulk
in the distance. Instead
of seeing you, we pause
and my eyes stray to the small
white butterfly whose wings
are caught in netted grass.

Pay Dirt

On my street of oaks and elms,
duplexes are gone to boarded
and secret insides, to the copper strippers,
mantel busters. Streets now canyons
where rivers run in a thin brown milk.
My house with its yellow pillars,
a sunroom where my grandmother
tended her African violets. Small petals
blooming in every season, even in this city
in Ohio where the sky was a leaden haze,
where the soot was called "pay dirt."

In the Cardiologist's Office

A *Whiter Shade of Pale* comes on a 70's musak version
and memory that unwelcomed guest visiting and staying
around too long wants to keep talking as I am waiting
for an echocardiogram a sonar picture of my heart
the thickness of the walls the synchrony of valves the slushing
of the beats and I am back there the night before the accident
by a lake. I see the moon hear the soft slap of water and the song
her face at first just ghostly turned a whiter shade of pale
and in the dark see his white teeth his long brown hair and feel
how uneasily he rides risk's edge and the next day the car hits us
on the Norton and he dies in the road and what I can say
about it is I keep his orange plaid shirt for thirty-nine years
his prayer beads from Korea, and the song when I hear it
and at first it is the pain the clenched neck muscles where I fell
against him then the dizziness *the room was humming harder*
as the ceiling flew away then just the dark weight of him
my hands circling his chest *spinning cartwheels cross the floor*
my head against his back bracing at the place where
the car crushed his heart.

Mayflies

On the downhill slope
they circle round

like the black flies of May,
bodies too small to swat.

Wind whisks them away
and then they circle back

to prick with their
anesthetic bite.

Mother in sepia brown,
color of sadness. Father

at the piano scaring the keys
and you, holding onto me.

For years we slept
on the old mattress

waking to the mill whistle
and the sulfurous dawn.

Our intentions grew together.
You went first and I said

I'm coming. You slid over,
my steps are slower.

Now moss, now slate, now stone.
Still the flies circling, doubling back.

Notes

Epigraphs_ "Kent State 1970" in the poem *Randomness* refers to the shooting of Sandra Scheuer who was shot wearing a red blouse on May 4, 1970 at Kent State; "The voting machines of Ohio" from *Patience* refers to the breakdown of the voting machines during the 2004 Ohio Presidential election; "That is what space is for" from Returning to Kent State, is from page 18 of Gaston Bachelard's, *The Poetics of Space*; *Fear's* epigraph concerns the setting of the concert in October after the shootings; the epigraph for *Undercover Dates* refers to the federal undercover operation on the campus after the shootings; "I was to keep her sitting next to me" in *The Paralegal* is from *Kent State Coverup*, by Joseph Kelner and James Munves, p.18; "The secret of this journey is to let the wind" in *The Accident*, is from lines 31 and 32 of *The Journey* by James Wright.

Lyrics_ "Worthy is the Lamb" and " He shall stand" from the libretto of the *Messiah* by Handel, words from the scriptures by Charles Jennens; "tear down the walls" from *We Can All Be Together* by Paul Kantner, Jefferson Airplane in Fear; lyrics in *In the Cardiologist's Office* are from *A Whiter Shade of Pale* by Procol Harum; lyrics from *Layla* in *Returning to Kent State* are by Eric Clapton.

The phrase, "small knots in the brain" in *Untying* is derived from the poem, *Having the Having*, line 1, " I tie knots in the strings of my spirit." From Jack Gilbert, *The Collected Works*.

Nancy Richardson's poems have appeared in journals and anthologies. Her first chapbook, *Unwelcomed Guest,* was published in 2013 and concerned coming of age in the rust-belt of Ohio and the shootings at Kent State University. *The Fire's Edge* extends that subject matter in elegies and reflections of living in that place and time. Nancy has an MFA in Writing from Vermont College where she focused on poetry in response to injustice. She has served on the Board of the Frost Place in Franconia, New Hampshire.

She has worked in government and education at the local, state, and federal levels as policy liaison to the Governor of Massachusetts and the U.S. Secretary of Education. Her work has focused on equal opportunity in education for all students, including those with disabilities. She holds a Master's Degree and a Doctorate in Education from Kent State University and a Master's Degree from Harvard University.

www.ingramcontent.com/pod-product-compliance
Lightning Source LLC
LaVergne TN
LVHW041509070426
835507LV00012B/1432